GOD SPOKE

Bridging the Sacred-Secular Divide with Divine Discourse

ERIK STRANDNESS, MD, MATh

WESTBOW PRESS®
A DIVISION OF THOMAS NELSON
& ZONDERVAN

Copyright © 2018 Erik Strandness, MD, MATh.

Cover Art by Keegan Strandness and Hope Thompson

All rights reserved. No part of this book may be used or reproduced by any means, graphic, electronic, or mechanical, including photocopying, recording, taping or by any information storage retrieval system without the written permission of the author except in the case of brief quotations embodied in critical articles and reviews.

This book is a work of non-fiction. Unless otherwise noted, the author and the publisher make no explicit guarantees as to the accuracy of the information contained in this book and in some cases, names of people and places have been altered to protect their privacy.

Scripture quotations are from The Holy Bible, English Standard Version (ESV), except where noted, copyright 2001 by Crossway, a publishing ministry of Good News Publishers. Used by permission. All rights reserved.

For information about my books or speaking engagements
visit my website at www.godsscreenplay.com

WestBow Press books may be ordered through booksellers or by contacting:

WestBow Press
A Division of Thomas Nelson & Zondervan
1663 Liberty Drive
Bloomington, IN 47403
www.westbowpress.com
1 (866) 928-1240

Because of the dynamic nature of the Internet, any web addresses or links contained in this book may have changed since publication and may no longer be valid. The views expressed in this work are solely those of the author and do not necessarily reflect the views of the publisher, and the publisher hereby disclaims any responsibility for them.

Any people depicted in stock imagery provided by Thinkstock are models, and such images are being used for illustrative purposes only.
Certain stock imagery © Thinkstock.

ISBN: 978-1-9736-1570-5 (sc)
ISBN: 978-1-9736-1569-9 (e)

Library of Congress Control Number: 2018901015

Print information available on the last page.

WestBow Press rev. date: 02/27/2018

I want to thank my family for their love and support during this project. I would also like to thank Keegan Strandness and Hope Thompson for the creative genius they put into the amazing cover. Finally, I would like to thank Rob and Kathy Mehl for editing my manuscript and fine-tuning it for publication. God bless you all.

CONTENTS

Chapter 1 Ghost in the Machine 1
Chapter 2 Soul Mate 14
Chapter 3 Speech Therapy 18
Chapter 4 Fact Checking 36
Chapter 5 Hearing Loss 45
Chapter 6 The Final Word 53

Endnotes 57

CHAPTER 1

Ghost in the Machine

Spirituality is one of the most common human experiences. Studies consistently show that 90 percent of all people believe in a god of some sort or another,[1] so the real question is not whether or not a god exists, but rather, Who is this god in whom most people believe? While we tend to think that atheism has been the biggest threat to our Christian faith, a 2017 poll from the Barna Group and Summit Ministries revealed that postmodernism and the new spirituality have actually had a greater impact.[2] While a small atheist minority continues to tell us that spirituality is just the inevitable high caused by years of mainlining the opiate of the masses, the rest of us continue to search for the cosmic drug lord. Spirituality, therefore, is not a demographic outlier but rather the statistically significant air we breathe. It is not a hobby for the scientifically illiterate but one of the basic elements in the periodic table of human experience. While debates with atheists can sharpen our faith, we need to remember that those people represent a very small worldview demographic, and with the exception of a small group of ardent nonbelievers, a denial of the spiritual realm is almost considered a human heresy. I would therefore argue that it makes more sense to begin our apologetic project by helping the majority identify their god rather than arguing with the minority about whether or not such a being exists.

The Bible gives us a clear example of this approach in the seventeenth chapter of Acts, when Paul visits Athens. As he entered the city, his spirit was provoked because he saw that it was full of idols. While the Athenians most likely believed that an abundance of altars revealed their religious wealth, Paul knew that it actually exposed their spiritual poverty. He began his discussion by congratulating them on their religious nature, but then he challenged them to get specific about who their god really was. He didn't let them off the hook with their "unknown god" defense but pushed them to "name Him and claim Him."

> So Paul, standing in the midst of the Areopagus, said, "Men of Athens, I perceive that in every way you are very religious. For as I passed along and observed the objects of your worship, I found also an altar with this inscription, 'To the unknown god.' What therefore you worship as unknown, this I proclaim to you." (Acts 17:22–23)

Most people we encounter will embrace a similarly vague type of spirituality. Our mission therefore is to help them know this unknown God. We need to begin by showing them that God is far too big to be placed under house arrest in tiny temples of their own creation, incarcerated by the limited religious conceptions of who they want Him to be. We need to point out that the reason they believe in a god in the first place is that they are His offspring. Sadly, they have been so busy creating Him in their own image that they haven't taken the time to look in the mirror and notice how much they resemble their Father.

> The God who made the world and everything in it, being Lord of heaven and earth, does not live in temples made by man, nor is he served by human hands, as though he needed anything, since he himself gives to all mankind life and breath and everything ... "'In him we live and move and have our being'; as even some of your own poets have said, 'For we are indeed his offspring.' Being then God's offspring, we ought not to think that the divine being is like gold or silver

> or stone, an image formed by the art and imagination of man." (Acts 17:24–25, 28–29)

Once we have their attention, we need to get real with them and tell them that their ignorance is no longer acceptable because God has already stepped into the world and made Himself known in the flesh. We can't let their cultural indifference go unchallenged because God is not a pastime but a person—not a fad but a Father. If we are sincere about helping people know the one true God, then we need to show them that not only does He exist but He is dying to meet them.

> The times of ignorance God overlooked, but now he commands all people everywhere to repent, because he has fixed a day on which he will judge the world in righteousness by a man whom he has appointed; and of this he has given assurance to all by raising him from the dead. (Acts 17:30–31)

Since the Athenians had no biblical background, Paul had to build his gospel presentation from the ground up by first appealing to their shared spiritual hunger and then feeding it with the bread of life. Our audience isn't much different from Paul's because we also live in a country that is largely biblically illiterate. There was a time in our past when Christianity was the bedrock of our nation and preaching was done to the choir, but times have changed, and we now find ourselves talking to the hymnally challenged. Our progressive biblical illiteracy has taken an even greater toll on our youth. The Pew Research Center, in its 2014 Religious Landscape Study, has shown that there is a steadily growing group of disenfranchised youth, or "nones," who have opted out of traditional church affiliations.[3] They continue to be spiritual but pursue it in unorthodox ways based largely on their personal feelings. The biggest threat to our young people, therefore, is not being told there is no God, but rather that there are multiple pathways to His doorstep—not atheism, but rather spiritual syncretism.

If the spiritual realm exists side by side with the physical world, then it would seem to me the height of foolishness to not take it seriously. Socrates said an unexamined life is not *worth living*, but I would add that failure to include the spiritual in that examination makes it not *worth dying for* either. Every worldview is driven by an insatiable desire to marry the physical and spiritual realms. Sadly, the wedding reception for most of them turns out to be a bust because they never bothered to get to know either the bride or the groom.

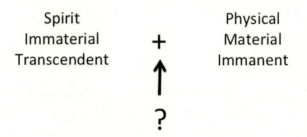

The Dilemma

We live on a planet inhabited by all sorts of physical objects, such as rocks, plants, and animals, yet among all this physicality, we find unique biological beings obsessed with spiritual fulfillment. We live in a world that is physical, material, and immanent, but we are haunted by the specter of a spiritual, immaterial, and transcendent realm. Instead of trying to create harmony between the two, we often take the path of least resistance and concentrate our energies in one or the other. Sadly, we end up with our human glasses half-empty and spend the rest of our lives thirsty.

The atheist takes the easy way out and tells us the spiritual realm doesn't exist. The Hindu takes the opposite tack and declares the physical world to be an illusion. The problem with both of these attempts at worldview oversimplification is that they don't match reality. The vast majority of humans recognize that the spiritual-physical question is not an either/or but rather a both/and proposition, and they spend most of their lives trying to combine the two into a seamless whole. Our inability to effectively combine these two spheres creates a sacred-secular divide in our lives—a division that treats the spiritual realm as a personal happy place to run to when the secular world becomes too overwhelming. Sadly, instead of taking the time to cultivate our spiritual gardens, we all too often throw up our hands and surrender to the thorns and thistles. We cannot dance with the devil for six days and then expect to exorcise our secular demons on Sunday. The good news is that Christianity is the only worldview capable of bringing them together in a way that satisfies both heart and mind.

When in Romans

> For what can be known about God is plain to them, because God has shown it to them. For his invisible attributes, namely, his eternal power and divine nature have been clearly perceived, ever since the creation of the world, in the things that have been made. So they are without excuse. (Romans 1:19–20)

St. Paul, in the first chapter of Romans, helps us bridge this gap by pointing out that there is an obvious ("plain to them") connection between a spiritual God ("his invisible attributes") and His physical creation ("the things that have been made"). He also makes it clear that the physical things we encounter are not accidental but intentional ("because God has shown it to them"), leaving every human being "without excuse" for not knowing God. People who frequent nature on a regular basis know that the physical world speaks to them in spiritual ways; therefore, it is no surprise that 90 percent of the population believe in a god of some sort or another. The very fact that we have a plethora of religions suggests that most people not only believe in this spirit but feel that this being must be revered. The problem is that most of them seem content with tipping their hats to the divine rather than taking time for a meet and greet.

"I'm a spiritual person." How often have you heard family, friends, and coworkers make that statement? Most people claim that they are spiritual, but when pushed for details they usually just recite a litany of vague feelings suggesting that there is more to life than just physical existence. So what exactly is it that they are experiencing?

> We all scour the seashore of discontent searching for something of value, something to give meaning and purpose to our lives. We pick up a beautiful seashell, hold it to our ear, and hear the rumblings of a restless roaring sea. We think we have found the elusive spirit that makes us truly human. Excited, we head to the beach party and share our find with friends. We sit around the fire and pass the shell around like a peace pipe, each human placing it next to his ear and smiling at the sounds of the untamed spiritual ocean beyond. The therapy session is then interrupted by one particularly astute young man who after listening intently peeks inside the shell and finds it empty. It appears that this self-help beach party was smoking more than peace. They had all fooled themselves into believing that this emptiness was actually a spiritual encounter. As we all know, misery loves company, so mankind rallies around the gaping spiritual hole in their lives, holding hands and chanting their "centering words," which in the end, only fills the empty chasm with groans of unhappiness rather than the contented sighs of the Holy Spirit.[4]

Sadly, we use the word *spiritual* to describe the dark, empty spaces left behind by our materialist presuppositions instead of as a way to describe a distinct entity intimately intertwined with the physical world. People prefer to live with a hazy notion of spirituality because they don't want a world where God is in control, yet they also don't want to be forced to robotically dance to the tune of their selfish genes. A vague understanding of spirituality gives them a culturally acceptable opt-out clause from a dreary world ruled by chemicals while simultaneously allowing them to define the terms of divine engagement.

Image Problem

In addition to the divine data we get from the natural world, we are struck by the fact that we humans also have a spiritual glow about us. We possess unique traits that are not found anywhere else on the planet and are compelled to look to the heavens to find the source. Humans are able to imagine and create things that never before existed. We recognize transcendent, universal moral laws. We are obsessed with finding purpose beyond basic survival. We treasure romance and not just seasonal, instinctual mating. We have the innate need to worship and are compassionate toward others. In the end, humans embody traits that are more consistent with Narnia than nature, which raises the question, "Why are we the only beings on the planet with this dual nature?"[5] The Bible perfectly explains this in the opening chapter of Genesis by revealing that we are created in the image of God. We are physical beings with spiritual traits. We are dust and breath.

Chemical Interlude

Most people are content with concentrating their energies in the physical world until a crisis arises that breaks their spirits. We see this dramatically displayed when our secular government asks the nation to pray for those afflicted by natural disaster. It appears that even our politicians know that when we reach our mortal limit, we have no choice but to turn to an immortal. The reason that there are no atheists in foxholes is because when physical death is on the line, we cry out for a spiritual medic. I would amend Vizzini's classic line from *The Princess Bride* and restate it as, "Never go in against [God] when death is on the line."

The atheist explains our spiritual nature as a psychological coping mechanism designed to pacify our fear of the unknown, but this explanation is problematic for several reasons. First of all, material creatures cannot step outside their materiality to conjure up a realm that doesn't exist. Chemicals are physical substances that have no conception of spirit; therefore, a material account of the world doesn't explain why the majority of people acknowledge a spiritual realm. Why would a bunch of chemicals come together for an eighty-year interlude obsessed with spiritual fulfillment and then settle for becoming cosmic compost? Second, creating a spiritual realm doesn't solve the problem of fear but actually compounds it by allowing us to imagine that there are monsters under our beds.

You cannot offer a spiritual explanation for our ignorance of the workings of the material world if Spirit doesn't exist. It is the scientific community's own "God-of-the-gaps" argument. They can't explain the overwhelming expression of spiritual feelings, so they offer a chemical spirit, which cannot be defended scientifically and, in the end, only provides more evidence that Spirit does, in fact, exist. They are appalled when religious people see the work of a personal God behind the construction of the world but then fail to see their own hypocrisy as they smuggle spiritual contraband into their material worldview to explain religion. In response, they would probably argue that if you get enough chemicals together, they will perform a séance and conjure up ghosts. The problem is that a plethora of proteins does not a pantheon make, and just because you bring a congregation of chemicals together in the human brain doesn't mean that they will have a religious revival. If you build a god with chemical Legos instead of divine Logos, then all you will have done is construct a toy for spiritually immature children.

I have practiced neonatal medicine for twenty years and seen firsthand the limits of science. I have seen glorious innovations developed on the research bench improve the care of neonates, but I have also seen many of these drugs, theories, and technologies fail miserably at the human bedside. Physicians are a skeptical lot. They have listened to an endless series of drug reps touting their latest drugs, basic scientists theorizing about disease processes, and biotech companies luring them into using the latest medical devices. Our skepticism of scientific innovation leads us to be even more skeptical when we hear a scientist play theologian or philosopher. If they can make mistakes in their own fields, why should we trust them to pontificate about things outside their areas of expertise? Science has helped me save many lives, yet it merely slinks away when it fails, leaving me without any tools to treat the spiritual mess left in its wake. Intensive care medicine heroically rides in on its white stallion to save the day, but all too frequently the callous black horseman of death follows in its tracks. The physician who loves the technological toys of neonatal medicine is now confronted with a puddle of toxic emotional mercury he or she doesn't know how to clean up.

I have been with many families as they mourned the loss of their babies. While the room is quiet as physical life ebbs away, the spiritual air is whipped up into a maelstrom of activity. *Why did God take my child? What have I done to deserve this? Is she in a better place? Is this God's will? Will I ever see her again?* Questions, like tornadoes, tear the roofs off of the parents' worldview homes, exposing them to the incessant beating of the *heavenly reign*. They weren't grieving over lost atoms or chemicals, because matter cannot mourn the loss of matter. They weren't lamenting dead neurotransmitters but rather lamenting the loss of a spirit that conducted them like a symphony. They did not shed tears because it was the end of the line for their selfish genes, but rather sobbed because a kindred spirit had moved away. How is it possible for purely physical beings to have a spiritual hemorrhage? A material thing cannot even conceive of a spiritual realm, so from where does it draw that information? My scientific textbooks never addressed these difficult spiritual questions; they just offered anesthetics to numb them. The beauty of the Bible is that it doesn't shy away from these queries but rather embraces them. Psalms, Job, Lamentations, and Ecclesiastes basically put a divine stamp of approval on the exploration of these complex spiritual issues. We can bury the body but can never bury the memories. The deceased may rest in peace, but the family has just begun years of spiritual unrest. Don't tell me humans are just chemicals or instincts. I have tested that idea out in the real world, and it doesn't work.

Erik Strandness, MD, MATh

Mind over Matter

> Today, there is a wide measure of agreement, which on the side of physics approaches almost to unanimity, that the stream of knowledge is heading towards a non-mechanical reality; the universe begins to look more like a great thought than like a great machine. Mind no longer appears as an accidental intruder into the realm of matter; we are beginning to suspect that we ought rather to hail it as the creator and governor of the realm of matter.[6]

Scientists are beginning to recognize that the prime reality in the universe is mind and not matter. They come to this conclusion because they find it difficult to look at the complexity of the world around them and not use words that imply thought. The more they explore the physical world, the more they recognize the oversight of an architect who has designed it to function as an ecologically integrated whole. Sadly, many scientists continue to reduce the world to chemical nails and wood and fail to see the larger biological house in which they live. They act like proud males who think they can put together a barbecue grill without first reading the instruction manual.

When I taught high school biology, I was struck by the inability of the textbook authors to express biological ideas without using terms that directly implied a mind. Words such as *design, engineer, blueprint, mechanism, fine-tune, architecture,* and *master plan* littered the pages, and yet astonishingly their conclusion was mindless materialism. The writers of these textbooks hypocritically used words that were not found in their evolutionary lexicons; confronted by a mind, they were forced to pull out an intelligent design thesaurus.

Through my medical practice, I have come to realize that this spiritual realm is more than just a sanctuary of grief; it is also a library of complex thoughts. As I treated disease and saved lives, I began to feel like I was a tinkerer in somebody else's workshop. I didn't create the factory in which I worked, but I seemed to be reading from its owner's manual. In medical school, we were required to understand normal anatomy and physiology before we could enter into the world of disease treatment and prevention. We assumed a standard existed before we even began our studies. The standard wasn't created by us but was rather assimilated through years of scientific discovery. Why would we assume a standard of body mechanics if we were haphazardly created on the evolutionary fly? My textbooks were objective repair manuals, not subjective Rorschach inkblots.

During my years of basic science research, I was amazed at how each newly discovered scientific truth opened up another layer of complexity. Rarely did laboratory discoveries become immovable, weight-bearing walls of scientific truth; rather, they became doors into rooms of ever-increasing complexity. It was as if scientists were looking deeper into a complex mind rather than uncovering a fortuitous series of genetic mistakes.

Archeologists sort through ancient rubble looking for evidence of human activity by searching for physical objects that have the marks of intelligence, such as cave paintings or pieces of stone fashioned into spear tips. In other words, they are searching for objects that defy natural explanation because they have been fashioned by a mind for a specific purpose. It appears that it doesn't take much evidence for an archeologist to recognize the work of a mind, yet many scientists studying the biological world see vastly more intricate levels of organization and complexity and stunningly attribute it to random chance.

When we purchase something that requires assembly, we first look at the picture of the final, functional product on the box. We then open the box and find it filled with intricately designed pieces that are useless on their own but form something far more complex when assembled together. In fact, one of the ways we recognize a mind is by its ability to create something unique from things that already exist. It may be an artist taking pigment and painting a picture or an engineer building a car from metal, but in either case, it is impossible to have something greater than its parts unless it is infused with the work of a mind.

In the neonatal intensive care unit (NICU), whenever I encountered babies with congenital anomalies, my first thought was that they had abnormalities in their genetic code. I recognized that the babies didn't match the typical baby "box-top picture" and wondered if there had been a mistake in the cellular instruction manual. In order to effectively practice medicine, a physician must acknowledge a standard human form composed of unique individual parts carefully integrated together into a well-oiled biological machine, because only then can they recognize when it fails to meet factory specifications. As a neonatologist, I recognize that a standard baby template exists that operates according to a preexisting instruction manual that I didn't write but must carefully read.

DNA is not just a random assembly of simple chemicals, but rather a medium of communication. It has intent and purpose and will accomplish that which it was designed to do. Randomness as a source of new information is absurd in the extreme. You cannot derive order from randomness because they are mutually exclusive. We all know this because we are pattern-seeking creatures, and the first pattern we seek is order. If I were to hand you a piece of paper with a grid of letters, you would immediately begin to look for a hidden sequence. However, if it turned out that those letters were actually random, you would soon discard the paper because it communicated nothing and was quite boring. Watson and Crick, the discoverers of DNA, knew they had found a submicroscopic code, yet they still couldn't see the elephant in the room: a code giver. While scientists tell us that the material universe began with a *physical singularity*, we must also account for the appearance of laws and information, which requires a *thought singularity*. A physical singularity begins with matter and energy, but information and laws begin with a mind.

In our human experience, information always implies communication or *knowledge in transit,* so when we encounter it, we need to ask ourselves what it is saying. Genetic information and natural laws aren't just amusing billboards on the side of life's highway but are actually stoplights controlling nature's traffic, and as we commute through our day-to-day lives, we can't help but marvel at the ingenuity of the "city planner." It is clear that life needs biological information, and *new* life needs new biological information. The Bible describes this perfectly by introducing us to a God who sequentially speaks new sentences of information into existence, and with each successive creative act adds ever-increasing layers of biological complexity. Creation is not just God's thought but also his thinking. God has not left the building but continues to offer his spoken word performances on weekends and holidays. He is not content admiring his collection of antique manuscripts but continues at his desk, pen in hand, *making all things new* (Rev 21:5). While the scientist tries to make the difficult case for a random word generator, the Bible offers a far more satisfactory personal God who speaks His mind.

As it turns out, the spirit we seek isn't a ghost haunting a machine, but rather a Creator in conversation. This is the essence of what Paul was communicating in the first chapter of Romans; God has filled the world with divine discourse and wants to strike up a conversation with humankind. The beauty of recognizing the mind as the prime reality is that the world becomes more than just a laboratory; it becomes a garden of the sublime where we encounter laws and literature, mechanisms and music, arithmetic and art. The poet and the philosopher, the singer and the scientist, the thespian and the theologian are all invited to pick God's brain. Exclusion of any would mean poverty for all.

While many people recognize that this spirit has a mind, what they really want to know is whether or not He cares about every sparrow that falls. Is He just a highly qualified mechanic, or is He also a trusted friend? Who is this mind anyway?

CHAPTER 2
Soul Mate

Personnel Department

While we want to treat the spiritual realm as a safe space to escape the stress of the world, we can't shake the feeling that someone already lives there. We try to dismiss Him as a vague essence but perpetually feel like He is looking over our shoulders. We are told that our lives are just the result of fate yet feel compelled to say "sorry" and "thank you." Despite our efforts to go it alone, we inevitably recognize that we need a divine hand up, and even though we may want Him to be a butler, we get this uncomfortable feeling that He is Lord of the manor.

    I would suggest that the reason we pursue spirituality is that, deep down, we know that it is not a physical tyrant who calls the shots but rather a spiritual overlord. Unable to define purpose, love, and morality on earthly terms, we instinctively look to the heavens. We sense that the traits that make us unique *persons* must have come from a unique *Person*. Interestingly, those traits, which we find inexplicable in material terms, are well understood in relational terms. Our cultural obsession with spirits and angels supports my contention that we believe the spiritual realm is personal. So when we engage in celestial seeking, we are not searching for the Force but rather a missing Person.

    Religions that offer vague spiritual essences as the ultimate reality have a hard time explaining why humans are so obsessed with personality. Even the nebulous Hindu Brahman or the Buddhist nirvana still incorporate middle-man bodhisattvas or avatars to give their spirituality some personality. The difference between religion in the East and religion in the West is that the West thinks primarily in terms of ongoing individuality and eternal personhood, while the East sees individual extinction and eternal nothingness. The problem with the Eastern mind-set, however, is that it cannot avoid the human need for personal relationship, and even though they speak of the unknowable Brahman or vague nirvana, they are forced to gain access to it through minor deities that have the attributes of personhood. They cannot escape the fact that any religious system that doesn't pay homage to human individuality is ultimately hollow. So when it comes to something as precious as our spirituality, we know that it must be based on relationship with a "person." This, however, is where the spiritual rubber meets the physical road because true relationship must be a two-way street, and we must be willing to woo as well as be wooed.

> You must have wondered why the enemy [God] does not make more use of His power to be sensibly present to human souls in any degree He chooses and at any moment. But you now see that the Irresistible and the Indisputable are the two weapons, which the very nature of His scheme forbids Him to use. Merely to over-ride a human will (as His felt presence in any but the faintest and most mitigated degree would certainly do) would be for Him useless. He cannot ravish. He can only woo.[7]

Let's take a look at how the original sin of wanting to be like God creates problems for us as we try to establish a relationship with this spiritual "person." We begin with a choice: we can either recognize the sheer otherness of our spiritual companion, or we can fudge and create our own doppelgangers. We can enter into a reciprocal relationship that is cemented with definable obligations or create a fictional friend whose "demands" come prepackaged with our own personal stamp of approval. We know we need an I–Thou relationship, but we keep bumping into our own egos. Sadly, we usually begin by opting for a god created in our own image. The problem with this approach is that once we have patted ourselves on the backs for effectively dealing with the spiritual elephant in the room, we hear our inner prophet get on his soapbox and proclaim, "You are that pachyderm." After being called out for our divine pretension, we take another tack and transform God into a vague nothingness, butterflies in the stomach, or perpetual puppy love. Once again we feel like we have achieved spirituality without obligation until our lives close up for business and we find ourselves *knock, knock, knockin' on heaven's door* only to have it opened by a God of consequence. The blurry God we kept at a distance now gets up in our grill, and what we saw only through a glass darkly is now seen face to face. It's easy to have an unknown God in your life but much more difficult when He knows your name.

> But now thus says the Lord, he who created you, O Jacob, he who formed you, O Israel: "Fear not, for I have redeemed you; I have called you by name, you are mine. (Isaiah 43:1)

God either is, or He is not, so any attempt to make Him into who we want Him to be is nothing but building an altar to our own divine pretension. Ultimately, after all of our religious searching, we will arrive at a place where we must make a commitment to this spiritual other. Will we take Him for better, for worse, for richer, for poorer, in sickness and in health, until death do us unite?

Interestingly, every religion, whether or not it recognizes a personal god, still thinks it is important to adhere to specific obligations in order to achieve spiritual communion. Islam and Christianity clearly have duties, but even the bland nothingness of Eastern religions still requires good karma and eightfold pathways. New-age religion, while lacking a rigorous salvation flow sheet, still focuses on acts of kindness, positive thoughts, and meditation as ways to establish a spiritual connection with the god within or the force without. All religions feel the need to create a template for spiritual relationship-building.

Spirit ⟶ Mind ⟶ Person ⟶ Relationship ?

Haunted Honeymoon

Accepting the fact that Spirit exists is an easy step for most people to take because they are constantly bombarded by feelings that they cannot attribute to chemicals alone. Taking it one step further and acknowledging that this spirit has a mind is also not a very difficult step because we constantly encounter the work of an artist, engineer, and mathematician in the world around us. However, the final step of accepting this spirit as a person is more difficult because it raises the troubling question of relationship commitment and responsibility. If we want to marry the spiritual and the physical, then we must know the rules of engagement. We can probably convince most people that spirit exists and that it has a mind, but if we want to take the Great Commission seriously, we need to be Christian matchmakers and bring them to the altar so they can at least look their spiritual groom in the eye and say "I do" or "I don't."

It's interesting that each religion not only encourages courtship of a spiritual soul mate but also offers an afterlife honeymoon. It turns out that what we want from spirituality is not a friend but a spouse. We don't want companionship; we want a lifelong marriage. The Hindu unites their atman with Brahman, the Buddhist dissolves into nirvana, the New Ager becomes magical cosmic dust, and the Christian is united with God at the wedding feast of the Lamb. If our relationship with this spirit ultimately ends in a marriage, then it would probably be a good idea to go on a few dates before we walk down that aisle. Is it possible to know anything about our future spiritual mate, or do we have to settle for an unknown mail-order bride?

CHAPTER 3
Speech Therapy

Look Who's Talking?

Now that we've established that spirit exists, has a mind, is personal, and requires a relationship, we need to ask ourselves how we can get to know one another. The good news is that spirituality isn't a blind date with the *unknown*, but rather courtship of the *known*. As St. Paul made clear, our first date begins with a stroll through His creational gallery.

What is it about the physical world that causes us to draw spiritual conclusions? I suspect that whenever we see beauty, design, and complexity in the world, we sense the presence of someone we cannot see yet feel compelled to engage with in conversation. All acts of worship, whether a church service, prayer, or meditation, are attempts to communicate with that mind. The question then becomes, which religious tradition actually explains our ability to strike up a conversation with the divine?

We recognize the work of a mind by observing the physical manifestation of its thoughts. We see a watch or a painting, and we detect the thoughts of an engineer or an artist. We hear a speech or listen to a song, and we detect the thoughts of an orator or musician. So what is the world saying that persuades us that there is a Creator? The Bible answers this question by introducing us to a God who speaks His mind. We cannot underestimate the importance of the three simple words, *And God said* … for understanding the connection between a spirit God and a physical world.

While Genesis is not the only Ancient Near Eastern (ANE) creation story, it is nonetheless absolutely unique. The other ANE myths describe a series of gods that arose from preexistent chaotic material who subsequently formed the rest of the world through conjuring acts, murder, and sexual promiscuity. For these cultures the universe was merely the fallout of the carnal behavior of their pantheon of ill repute. Genesis, on the other hand, introduces us to a single God who intentionally creates a very good world through orderly acts of speech and then forms beings capable of understanding what He has spoken. The world that had been deaf to His words before humans were created was filled with beings capable of engaging in conversation. Creation stories from the ANE have become nothing but historical curiosities because they tell us nothing about the world in which we live. Genesis, on the other hand, continues to be relevant because it actually describes the world we experience every day of our lives. *We are still talking about Genesis because Genesis is still talking about us.* While there are many substantial differences between the Genesis account and other ANE creation stories, the most profound is the introduction of a God who speaks creation into being.

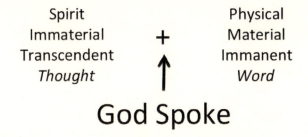

By the word of the Lord the heavens were made, and by the breath of his mouth all their host. (Psalm 33:6)

Speak to Me

As a scientist, I want evidence that a spirit can communicate with a physical world; I want proof that something immaterial can be manifested in a material way; I want to be sure that the transcendent can be known in the immanent. The good news is that we have seen this phenomenon demonstrated for millennia but have taken it for granted because it is so commonplace. What am I talking about? Human speech. Speech begins with an immaterial thought in the mind. That immaterial thought is then converted into physical form by taking the air in our lungs and forcing it across vocal cords, vibrating the air, and sending out physical sound waves. Those sound waves are then received by the eardrum of another person, sent to the brain, and reconverted into the same immaterial thought. Magically, an immaterial thought becomes a physical reality and then is reconverted into the same immaterial thought in the mind of another. A thought cannot be surgically removed from a brain or formed by mixing chemicals together in a test tube because it has no physical essence, and yet, in the act of communication, ideas take on physical form. Stunningly, the Bible introduces us to a spirit God who spoke a physical universe into existence; His immaterial thought became physical words and filled the universe with divine discourse. As it turns out, God has always had the world on His mind.

> "The most incomprehensible thing about the universe is that it is comprehensible."[8]

Einstein was stunned that the universe could be measured and represented in mathematical formulas, but that comes as no surprise to those of us who know that God isn't just a flower arranger but also an engineer.

> Who has measured the waters in the hollow of his hand and marked off the heavens with a span, enclosed

the dust of the earth in a measure and weighed the mountains in scales and the hills in a balance? (Isaiah 40:12)

God not only spoke words, but those words became sentences, those sentences became paragraphs, those paragraphs became chapters, and those chapters made up the greatest story ever told. Each word was like a "good" note in a larger "very good" symphony performed for an audience of image bearers capable of tapping their feet to His melody. We can look at a sunrise, a fir tree, and an elephant and instinctively know that they are "good words" that fit together into a larger ecological "very good" whole. When we look at the world around us, we don't see evolutionary works in progress but rather a collection of finished masterpieces.

> And God said … And God saw that it was good. (Genesis 1)
> And God saw everything that He had made and behold it was very good. (Genesis 1:31)

Since the physical world represents God's thoughts, we can better appreciate why Paul told us that God's *invisible attributes* could be known through *the things that have been made.* Similar to the way in which we know the thoughts of another human being through speech, we can know God's thoughts through the physical manifestation of His spoken words. When we hear a babbling brook, we are actually eavesdropping on a stream of divine thought.

> The Heavens declare the glory of God,
>   and the sky above proclaims his handiwork.
> Day to day pours out speech,
>   and night to night reveals knowledge.
> There is no speech, nor are there words,
>   whose voice is not heard.
> Their voice goes out through all the earth,
>   and their words to the end of the world. (Psalm 19:1-4)

> But ask the beasts, and they will teach you;
>> the birds of the heavens, and they will tell you;
> or the bushes of the earth, and they will teach you;
>> and the fish of the sea will declare to you.
> Who among all these does not know
>> that the hand of the Lord has done this?
> In his hand is the life of every living thing
>> and the breath of all mankind. (Job 12:7-10)

While we often think of God's creation as *ex nihilo* (out of nothing), I think it is more helpful to think of it as *ex cogitatio* (out of thought). If we just focus on God creating the universe out of nothing, we miss the far more profound biblical truth that the world is comprehensible because it started out as God's thought. Since God spoke His mind, we find beauty, information, order, and complexity in the world. Nature then becomes the common language we share with God and every other human being on the planet, which is a *very good* place to begin to build a biblical view of the world.

Celestial Conversation

God spoke the universe into being, but those were not His first words. God exists in three persons; therefore, the Godhead has always been in eternal trialogue. The Father is perfect thought, the Holy Spirit is perfect speech, and Jesus is the perfect Word. Thankfully, God let us in on the conversation by literally *fleshing out* His thought. God had to raise His Jesus voice in order to get our attention but then commissioned the Holy Spirit to whisper words of encouragement in our ears so that He could finish His work in us.

If Father, Son, and Holy Spirit are all talking around the Trinitarian table then it would appear that conversation is a key component of what it means to be an image bearer. In fact, in Genesis one, just before humans are created, we are allowed to eavesdrop on a celestial conversation, "Let *us* make man in *our* image, after *our* likeness" (Gen 1:26). Once the Godhead had reached an accord, we find that the first step in creating image bearers was to make them male and female - it appears that image bearing is most powerfully represented by two humans capable of striking up a conversation. The importance of bantering beings was further amplified in the second chapter of Genesis when God acknowledged that it was not good for Adam to be alone with his thoughts. God then paraded animals before Adam to show him that it was only possible to have a *very good* conversation with a being that was his image bearing intellectual equal. God made it clear that thinking, talking, and listening were intimately tied to what it meant to be created in God's image. While the sound of one hand clapping may be an interesting koan for the isolated meditation of a Zen Buddhist, it appears that it takes two to tango if one wants to bear the image of God.

Is Anybody Listening?

While every conversation must begin with a speaker, it also requires a listener. Effective communication occurs only when the person with whom we are speaking has something in common with us such that he or she is capable of rethinking our original thought. When I speak to my cat, the most I can expect is some form of behavior modification, but when I speak with another human being, I can share an intellectual intimacy. I can invite that person into my mind to explore the immaterial essence of who I am.

> "If a tree were to fall on an island where there were no human beings, would there be any sound?"[9]

We can expand this thought experiment and ask ourselves, *If God spoke and there were no human beings to hear, would there be any speech?* Not wanting His words to fall on deaf ears, God created beings that share His image, beings capable of rethinking His thoughts after Him. In the Genesis creation account, it was not until humans were created that God declared the world to be *very good*. Is it possible that what makes creation very good is the presence of beings capable of hearing and understanding what He has spoken?

> When I look at your heavens, the work of your fingers,
>   the moon and the stars, which you have set in place,
> what is man that you are mindful of him,
>   and the son of man that you care for him? (Psalm 8:3-4)

If God was content to just make stuff, then any magical trick would suffice, but Genesis reveals a God who not only spoke His mind but also made beings capable of appreciating His creational rhetoric. If this is true, then what makes for an appropriate audience?

> Then God said, "Let us make man in our image, after our likeness. And let them have dominion over the fish of the sea and over the birds of the heavens and over the livestock and over all the earth and over every creeping thing that creeps on the earth." So God created man in his own image, in the image of God he created him; male and female he created them. (Genesis 1:26–27)

In order to communicate with another person, we need to have something in common. Humans are able to understand what God has spoken because they are *image bearers*. I would argue that one of the main attributes of an image bearer is divine voice recognition software. God fashioned us in such a way that we are the only beings on the planet capable of understanding the words He spoke into creation. In fact, scientists are discovering that humans are "intuitive theists," creatures who, from a very early age, recognize a God.[10] I would argue that "intuitive theist" is really just a scientific way of describing an image bearer. It appears that fluency in God-speak begins at a very young age because our ability to perceive God is programmed into normal human development just like walking and talking. The fact that it appears to be such an important milestone should cause us to ask if promoting atheism is in fact a form of sociological malpractice.

Children as young as four and five years of age already possess a fairly advanced "natural religion" that develops independently of their cultural upbringing.[11] I find it quite remarkable that both the Bible and science confirm that our ability to recognize God is hardwired into what it means to be human. When we evangelize another person, we are in essence preaching to the choir because we are speaking to a being prewired to sing God's praises. The scientific literature would suggest that every atheist is actually born a believer but then makes the decision to turn off his or her voice recognition software because it interferes with the ability to fall in love with the sound of their own voice.

> For you formed my inward parts;
> > you knitted me together in my mother's womb.
> I praise you, for I am fearfully and wonderfully made.
> > Wonderful are your works;
> > my soul knows it very well.
> My frame was not hidden from you,
> > when I was being made in secret,
> > intricately woven in the depths of the earth.
> Your eyes saw my unformed substance;
> > in your book were written, every one of them,
> > the days that were formed for me,
> > when as yet there were none of them.
> *How precious to me are your thoughts, O God!*
> > *How vast is the sum of them!*
> *If I would count them, they are more than the sand.*
> > *I awake, and I am still with you.* (Psalm 139:13-18, emphasis added)

> You have multiplied, O Lord my God,
> > your wondrous deeds and your *thoughts* toward us;
> > none can compare with you!
> I will proclaim and tell of them,
> > yet they are more than can be told. (Psalm 40:5, emphasis added)

> How great are your works, O Lord!
> Your *thoughts* are very deep! (Psalm 92:5, emphasis added)

The Hebrew word for "listen" is *shema*. It is a far more powerful word than our limited English translation allows. *Shema* means to not only listen but to contemplate and act[12]; therefore, when God calls us to listen, He is also calling us to take what He has said seriously. God's speech isn't the word of the day but rather the words of eternal life.

> Simon Peter answered him, "Lord, to whom shall we go? You have the words of eternal life, and we have believed, and have come to know, that you are the Holy One of God." (John 6:68–69)

Lingua Dei

A common image alone is not enough for communication to be effective; we must also share a common language. The words we use when we speak must have the same meaning for the listener. God spoke in the common language of the people, a *lingua franca*, if you will; therefore, we have no excuse for not understanding what He has said. I think it is more appropriate to describe this as a *lingua Dei* because it originated in the mind of God. I find it quite interesting that one of the most difficult human attributes for evolutionary science to explain is language, yet from a biblical perspective, beings capable of complex speech, created in the image of a speaking God, makes perfect sense.

> One distinctive feature about humans is the language capacity. It's central for our present existence and it doesn't seem to have anything analogous or homologous to other organisms. It seems unique to the human species, it's essential and it's also uniform across the species.[13]

Language defies evolutionary explanation, yet is one of the key biblical attributes of an image bearer. While the world around us is composed of the words of God, we need to remember that humans were also spoken into existence and therefore have a working knowledge of what it means to be God-breathed. Since we are both dust and breath, we hear God speak in the physical world around us as well as the spiritual world within us.

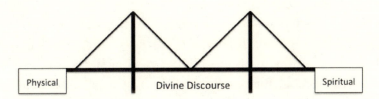

Since God spoke, a bridge of divine discourse spans the gap between the physical and spiritual realm, and our once-perilous leap into the unknown becomes a simple commute across the verbally known. As it turns out, the gap separating us from God is not filled with deathly silence but rather the words of life.

> God spoke, therefore I am.
> I hear, therefore God is.

Pancake House on the Edge of Totality

> He is the radiance of the glory of God and the exact imprint of his nature, and he upholds the universe by the word of his power. (Hebrews 1:3)

The book of nature continues to be a bestseller because God continues to read from its pages. He begins the day with an opening-line sunrise and concludes with a sunset exclamation point. He makes the "going out of the morning and the evening to shout for joy" (Psalm 65:8). God's story is an ongoing liturgy of nature, and if we listen closely, we can hear His daily homily reminding us that we walk on hallowed ground. Sadly, instead of carefully listening to God sing His creational hymns, we often use our outside voices and drown Him out with our own secular soliloquy. We insert our human voice into God's screenplay, and the world ends up looking like a badly overdubbed martial arts film.

A good friend of mine drove from Seattle, Washington, to Madras, Oregon in 2017 in order to witness a total eclipse of the sun firsthand. The traffic was terrible because thousands of her closest friends had the same idea. On the last part of her trip, she and her friends arose early in the morning in order to find a good viewing spot, and when they arrived, they stopped for breakfast at a pancake house. She dubbed the restaurant "The Pancake House on the Edge of Totality," which is a pretty heady title for a breakfast establishment but yet quite appropriate considering its location in relation to the impending event. This rare meteorological phenomenon caught the attention of the world and prompted many sane people to take a break from their humdrum lives to see a rock pass in front of a star. They undertook hours of preparation and travel all to witness darkness in the daytime, a phenomenon that is quite easily replicated by an afternoon nap. I find it absolutely remarkable that this event drew the attention of millions of people from every country throughout the world. It spoke the same language to everyone, no matter his or her culture or ethnicity. It was well attended not because it was a unique physical event but because it offered a front-row seat at a divine spoken-word performance.

Recurrent natural phenomena such as sunrises and sunsets, the seasons, and the tides are designed to synchronize our lives with God's words. He reminds us to set our spiritual watches by the recurrent pealing of His natural bell. He embedded predictability into nature not to create mindless routine but to bring Him back to mind. One of the consistent themes in the Bible is God's call to remember, remember, remember. Thankfully, He makes it easy on us by meeting us in the sun and the rain, the morning and the evening, and the fall and the spring. We should be grateful that God continues to schedule meetings with us in His daily planner because we all too often forget to show up. How sad that despite being surrounded by divine discourse, we often don't hear a *word* He says.

Walking the Mystery

> He has made everything beautiful in its time. Also, he has put eternity into man's heart, yet so that he cannot find out what God has done from the beginning to the end. (Ecclesiastes 3:11)

It is important to remember that this bridge is not only paved with what God has said but also by what He has left unsaid, a stretch of road that is not silent, but rather filled with God's unspoken thoughts. I emphasize this because many people find mystery to be the most intriguing connection between God and humankind. As mortal, finite beings, we cannot wrap our minds around eternity, yet God places it in our hearts. As Paul said, the natural world causes us to recognize a God in the universe, but it is our spiritual nature that inspires us to ask what He is thinking. While most of us travel the solid ground of divine discourse, a certain group of gifted humans loves to walk the mystery. The painter, writer, and musician are so uniquely gifted that they are able to hear what God has left unspoken—unique humans capable of peeking behind the veil for a brief moment and giving us a sketch of what they saw. Just because it's a mystery doesn't mean that it isn't solid ground. When we evangelize others, we must respect both the certain and the sublime because many people prefer to walk the mystery rather than take the apologetic bus.

> Take a moment to let the significance of this send shivers down your spine. This universe has within its vast swirling wisps of scattered elements a fixed number of connecting points between the immense realm of the things and the infinite realm of thoughts. You know this because one of these connecting points

is humming with activity right now, inside your skull, enabling you to reconstruct thoughts from physical symbols on paper or on an electronic display ... These connecting points are the places—the only places—where the world of atoms and the world of ideas are made to shake hands. Poet meets muse. Sculptor touches stone. Melody finds strings. Ideas flow to paper. Thirst is quenched. Loneliness ended.[14]

Divine Discourse

We have discussed God's speech in a very general sense, but what is He actually saying? The good news is that His creative speech has been compiled in the book of nature, the first volume in His *word*, *Word*, *WORD* trilogy. It is a literary work that reveals God's spirit through its physical pages. It tells us that the world is composed of good parts put together in a very good way. It describes a beautiful world of order and complexity inhabited by special animals and unique humans. We get the sense that it was once perfect, providing us with an idyllic standard by which we are able to judge the state of the world. It fills us with an internal garden optimism but also alerts us to the fact that something has gone horribly wrong in the wilderness. The natural world actually raises more questions than it answers, and we are left wondering how to make sense of it all. Every worldview acknowledges the book of nature but then tries to build a larger metanarrative around those unanswered questions. They are drawn into the drama, but instead of letting it unfold, they arrogantly take the pen from the Creator and write the rest of the story themselves. The good news for Christians is that God wasn't done talking after He recited the book of nature. He also commissioned image-bearing beings to become inspired spokespeople and scripturally fill in the rest of the details. Once again, God's immaterial thought became a physical reality but this time through the inspired written word of His image bearers. The questions raised by the creational *words* found in the book of nature are completely answered by His inspired scriptural *Word*.

The Bible is a survival manual that helps us navigate the wilderness and directs us to our true home. We know it is reliable because it is the only book that accurately describes the world in which we live. Since it flawlessly maps out the landscape of life, we can trust it to guide us on our journey to the new heaven and earth. We stand in awe of God's *eternal power and divine nature* when we read the book of nature but are then prompted to turn the page and meet Him in Holy Scripture. The creatively spoken *words* of God are illuminated by the *Word* of God and direct us to the ultimate source of that light, the incarnate *WORD*.

> For the word of God is living and active, sharper than any two-edged sword, piercing to the division of soul and of spirit, of joints and of marrow, and discerning the thoughts and intentions of the heart. (Hebrews 4:12)

> But as for you, continue in what you have learned and have firmly believed, knowing from whom you learned it and how from childhood you have been acquainted with the sacred writings, which are able to make you wise for salvation through faith in Christ Jesus. All Scripture is breathed out by God and profitable for teaching, for reproof, for correction, and for training in righteousness, that the man of God may be competent, equipped for every good work. (2 Timothy 3:14–17)

We often speak of the book of nature and the Bible as two independent sources of testimony about God, but Paul considered them a seamless whole. I would argue that they are not two separate books at all, but rather the preface and narrative of the greatest story ever told. Since our culture is becoming less biblically literate, even among evangelicals, the traditional apologetic appeal to scripture is falling on deaf ears. We need to once again reacquaint people with God's natural world preface so that they will be curious enough to open up the Good Book. Since everyone understands God's common grace where "He makes his sun rise on the evil and on the good, and sends rain on the just and on the unjust" (Mt 5:45) we have been given a wonderful opportunity to stand with our fellow humans in the sun and rain and talk apologetically about the weather. Talking to others about God doesn't involve teaching them a strange new language but rather introducing them to the One whose words they already know. If we can get them intrigued by God's preamble, then we can get them to turn the page and read *the rest of the story*. We need to remember that general revelation only sets the scene for the story, but it is God's saving revelation in sacred scripture that actually drives the performances on the world stage.[15]

As we all know, a picture is worth a thousand words; therefore, the problem isn't a lack of creational text, but rather its proper translation. The book of nature presents us with the *words* God spoke into creation. The Fall resulted in distortion of those *words* through the devilish appropriation of sinful syntax. The scriptural *Word* helps us recover the meaning of those created *words*. Finally, the *WORD* made flesh restores God's original garden grammar, and our newfound literacy compels us to hit the Great Commission road to get the *WORD* out. Maybe it would be more appropriate for us to speak of a Christian *Word*view rather than *world*view.

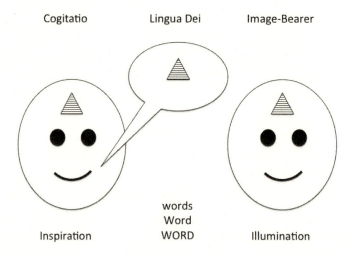

First Responders

God made it clear that His words would not return to Him empty, so He created beings that would be mouthpieces of praise for the planet. God was not content to just have His words heard; He also wanted a response. Humans are God's first responders. The traffic across the bridge of divine discourse is therefore a two-way street. God speaks, humans hear, and then they offer back praise and worship. Interestingly, God declares His creation very good only after He has formed beings in His image. As I mentioned before, it may be that what takes the planet to this "very good" level are creatures capable of responding to His spoken word. God's speech isn't an algorithm for automatons but interlocution with an image bearer. Free will, therefore, becomes the choice between dialoguing with the divine or loving the sound of our own mutinous murmurings.

> For my thoughts are not your thoughts,
> > neither are your ways my ways, declares the Lord.
>
> For as the heavens are higher than the earth,
> > so are my ways higher than your ways
> > and my thoughts than your thoughts.
>
> "For as the rain and the snow come down from heaven
> > and do not return there but water the earth,
> > making it bring forth and sprout,
> > giving seed to the sower and bread to the eater,
>
> so shall my word be that goes out from my mouth;
> > it shall not return to me empty,
> > but it shall accomplish that which I purpose,
> > and shall succeed in the thing for which I sent it. (Isaiah 55:8-11)

What does the Bible mean when it states that God's words shall not return to Him empty? Does He want to hear a transcript of His inaugural creation speech, or is He more interested in listening to the analysis of the human press corps? If He just wanted to hear an echo of His own words, He would have created an empty world with better acoustics, but instead He chose to fill it with sound-absorbing creatures capable of offering His words back in an astonishing array of human aesthetic. We have all engaged in divine word detailing, but sadly most of us fail to postmark our gifts back to God and end up hoarding His praise. Thinking we are collecting rare pieces of human genius, we end up bottling up the human response to the sacred. Instead of worshipping the Creator, we venerate the created, and our art exhibits become studios of self-adulation rather than galleries of godly gratitude.

When we return God's words to Him, they can be in the form of worship, work, art, or education. When we think of all the ways humans make this planet unique, we quickly realize that when confronted by God's words, we actually have a lot to say back. I believe that God created each of us unique so that when His voice goes out, the words we subsequently offer back to Him are uniquely embellished with our own personal interpretations of what He has said. He gives us a natural lexicon and then bids us to write Him a love letter; a cow becomes a latte, a tree becomes a boat, and a plant becomes a cure for cancer. Just like we love to see the world through our children's eyes, I believe that God loves to see His world through our eyes.

In the beginning, God created ... The first words of the Bible reveal a God who is at heart a Creator. He is a painter, potter, and performer. He hovered over His easel and raised His brush, and a dark canvas exploded in a big bang of Technicolor. He took a formless lump of clay, spun it on His potter's wheel, and sculpted a planet. He spoke a majestic monologue into the empty void, and His voice returned a dialogue full of life. In order to make sure His symphonic soliloquy didn't fall on deaf ears, He created beings equipped with divine voice recognition software. He filled the planet with image-bearing art patrons capable of creatively embellishing His divine words and returning them back to Him in a chorus of praise.

Beauty is in the eye of the beholder not because beauty is relative but because it is experienced uniquely by every being created in God's image. He delights when image-bearing artists-in-training embellish His creative words and offer them back in a dizzying array of imaginative praise. Our individual responses to God's world are like unique pieces of art adorning His Edenic sanctuary, adding inimitable optical nuance to the heavenly feng shui. As He walks the hallways, He sees familiar pieces of His own work embroidered with a distinctively human touch and smiles because He knows that imitation is the sincerest form of flattery.

The light God first called into being served as stage lighting for the unfolding universe, but once it lit upon His image-bearing prisms, it was refracted into a rainbow of praise. We have a choice: we can stand in the spotlight and take a bow, or we can offer back a performance of image-bearing wonder. We can let His spoken words pile up like junk mail at our doors, or we can artistically respond to every word, repackage it, and mark it "Return to Sender."

> I cannot conceive the necessity for God to love me, when I feel so clearly that even with human beings affection for me can only be a mistake. But I can easily imagine that he loves that perspective of creation, which can only be seen from the point where I am.[16]

CHAPTER 4

Fact Checking

What Is Truth?

In this day and age, we are bombarded with all kinds of information. We find incredible reports on the Internet and ask ourselves whether or not it is fake news. We check to see if political speeches pass the sniff test by seeing how many "Pinocchios" the fact-checkers have awarded. While our skepticism often leaves us despondent, it also reveals just how important finding truth is to the human mind. It is perfectly appropriate to ask such questions because doing so forms the basis of how we properly navigate the world. Since we expect people to speak the truth, we wouldn't expect anything less from the God of the universe. He calls us to worship Him in spirit and truth, which means that He would be disappointed if we didn't investigate His claims. But how do we know that what God has spoken is true? We must first begin by asking, *What is truth?*

> Conformity of the intellect and the thing.[17]

> The correspondence between what one thinks, believes, or opines and what actually exists.[18]

Truth is the immaterial unity of physical diversity. It is the transcendent glue that holds the immanent together. We insist something is true when it rises above its individual components and becomes universally applicable. If truth is the correspondence of thought and reality, then God's truth should be the perfect correspondence of His thought to the physical world. God spoke; therefore, His speech is available to everyone, and we are left without any excuse for not fact-checking what He has said. As we read the book of nature, we are prompted to ask spiritual questions, which is another way of saying we want to know God's thoughts on the *matter*. Every religion has a holy book that its believers claim reveals the mind of their god or gods, but which one actually corresponds to the world the way we experience it? Eastern religions posit an ultimately unknowable god, which makes it very difficult to discern what that god is thinking. New-age religions make God either a force that bends to the will of humankind or the god within that must be awakened; in either case, truth becomes what humans want it to be. The Judeo-Christian God, however, is a God who speaks His mind and continues to leave a paper trail that we can follow to verify His truth claims.

In Genesis, God put His stamp of approval on His physically manifested thought by declaring it "very good" (Gen 1:31). We can therefore summarize God's truth as the *very good* benediction He offered when He finished His creational speech.

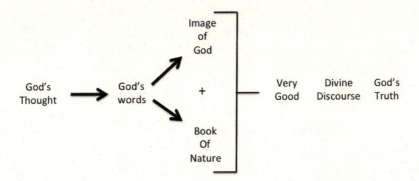

> Jesus said to her, "Woman, believe me, the hour is coming when neither on this mountain nor in Jerusalem will you worship the Father. You worship what you do not know; we worship what we know, for salvation is from the Jews. But the hour is coming,

and is now here, when the *true worshipers will worship the Father in spirit and truth,* for the Father is seeking such people to worship him. *God is spirit, and those who worship him must worship in spirit and truth.*" The woman said to him, "I know that Messiah is coming (he who is called Christ). When he comes, he will tell us all things." Jesus said to her, "I who speak to you am he." (John 4:21–26, emphasis added)

Jesus tells the Samaritan woman that real worship consists of recognizing the correspondence of God's thought to His created world and then living in a way consistent with that knowledge. But how are we to discern God's truth and evaluate whether or not His thoughts match physical reality?

Wisdom

The Bible tells us that we must seek wisdom in order to understand the proper connection between God's thoughts and His created world. Wisdom is not measured by level of education, SAT scores, academic awards, or publications but by the number of wrinkles and gray hairs we have accumulated during our life journeys. Wisdom is found in someone whose life has been a series of personal experiments conducted under the frequently harsh conditions of the world's laboratory and whose findings are not just theories but actual data. Wisdom is frequently acquired at a higher life price than any college tuition. We seek out wise people to help us see things that our limited experience prevents us from seeing. Our search for sage advice usually leads us to the elderly because they have already spent a lifetime trying to match reality to their own thoughts and concluded that life makes sense only when they surrender their pride and align their world to God's thoughts. Our search for truth is no different because we must also turn to the Ancient of Days for guidance, but the good news is that He has already incorporated wisdom into His created order so we don't have to look far before we gain insight.

The Lord by wisdom founded the earth;
> by understanding he established the heavens;
by his knowledge the deeps broke open,
> and the clouds drop down the dew. (Proverbs 3:19-20)

"The Lord possessed me at the beginning of his work,
> the first of his acts of old.
Ages ago I was set up,
> at the first, before the beginning of the earth.
When there were no depths I was brought forth,
> when there were no springs abounding with water.
Before the mountains had been shaped,
> before the hills, I was brought forth,
before he had made the earth with its fields,
> or the first of the dust of the world.
When he established the heavens, I was there;
> when he drew a circle on the face of the deep,
when he made firm the skies above,
> when he established the fountains of the deep,
when he assigned to the sea its limit,
> so that the waters might not transgress his command,
> when he marked out the foundations of the earth,
> *then I was beside him, like a master workman,*
>> *and I was daily his delight,*
>> *rejoicing before him always,*
> *rejoicing in his inhabited world*
>> *and delighting in the children of man.* (Proverbs 8:22-31, emphasis added)

One of the most fascinating aspects of God's creative process is the integration of wisdom into the construction of the universe. Proverbs describes wisdom as being at God's side from the beginning like a master craftsman. God *delighted* as wisdom became a part of His creative endeavor. Wisdom is described as *rejoicing* before God and *rejoicing* in the inhabited world. The Hebrew word for "rejoice," *sachaq*, can also be translated as *play* or *laugh*;[19] therefore, God delighted when wisdom began to joyously participate in the inhabited world. Interestingly, wisdom also felt delight when humans recognized her place in God's created order.

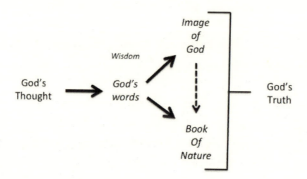

True wisdom, therefore, is the ability to hear God's words, rethink His thoughts, and live in a way consistent with that knowledge. Once we seek God's wisdom, we will be brought into all truth. But how do we obtain wisdom?

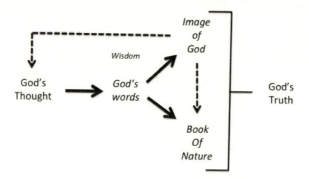

And I, when I came to you, brothers, did not come proclaiming to you the testimony of God with lofty speech or wisdom. For I decided to know nothing among you except Jesus Christ and him crucified. And I was with you in weakness and in fear and much trembling, and my speech and my message were not in plausible words of wisdom, but in demonstration of the Spirit and of power, that your faith might not rest in the wisdom of men but in the power of God. Yet among the mature we do impart wisdom, although it is not a wisdom of this age or of the rulers of this age, who are doomed to pass away. But we impart a secret and hidden wisdom of God, which God decreed before the ages for our glory. None of the rulers of this age understood this, for if they had, they would not have crucified the Lord of glory. (1 Corinthians 2:1-8)

Fear Factor

The Bible makes it clear that wisdom is obtained through fear of the Lord, but what is fear? Biblical fear is defined as awe, respect, reverence, and terror. In essence, it is the humility to admit that despite what the serpent said, we will never be like God.

> The fear of the Lord is the beginning of wisdom,
> and the knowledge of the Holy One is insight. (Proverbs 9:10)

Why is fear necessary for obtaining wisdom? It is only when we are acutely aware of God's *eternal power and divine nature* that we can set aside our pride and accept the fact that something greater than us exists. If we believe we are the smartest people in the room, then we will be deaf to the words of the cosmic genius. If we are not awed by the immensity, complexity, order, and beauty of the universe, then we will never seek the One who spoke it into existence. True fear ultimately comes down to accepting the fact that we live in God's world and He doesn't live in ours.

> By the word of the Lord the heavens were made,
> and by the breath of his mouth all their host.
> He gathers the waters of the sea as a heap;
> he puts the deeps in storehouses.
> *Let all the earth fear the Lord;*
> *let all the inhabitants of the world stand in awe of him!*

For he spoke, and it came to be;
> *he commanded, and it stood firm.* (Psalm 33:6-9, emphasis added)

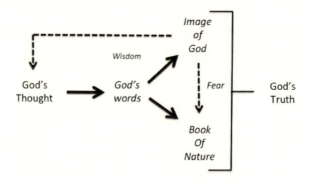

Job is a prime example of fear leading to wisdom. Job experienced a great deal of tragedy in his life, which he felt was undeserved. He had some serious questions about what had happened and received little help from his friends, so he sought answers from God Himself. Once God granted Job an audience, He began the discussion by making it clear who was in charge of the universe. God knew that Job could only become wise if he truly feared the Lord; therefore, He presented Job with His cosmic resume. Before Job could understand God's wisdom, He had to be humbled.

> Then the Lord answered Job out of the whirlwind and said:
> "Who is this that darkens counsel by words without knowledge?
> Dress for action like a man;
> > I will question you, and you make it known to me.
> "Where were you when I laid the foundation of the earth?
> > Tell me, if you have understanding.
> Who determined its measurements—surely you know!
> > Or who stretched the line upon it?
> On what were its bases sunk,
> > or who laid its cornerstone. (Job 38:1-6)

When God was done speaking, Job understood the fear of the Lord, and while he didn't get the answer he wanted, he got the wisdom he needed. Job was frustrated because he wanted reality to conform to his own thoughts, but once he began to fear God, he acquired the wisdom necessary to recognize that the world actually conformed to God's thoughts, and it was then that he was brought into all truth.

> Then Job answered the Lord and said:
> "I know that you can do all things,
>   and that no purpose of yours can be thwarted.
> 'Who is this that hides counsel without knowledge?'
>   Therefore I have uttered what I did not understand,
>   things too wonderful for me, which I did not know.
> 'Hear, and I will speak;
>   I will question you, and you make it known to me.'
> I had heard of you by the hearing of the ear,
>   but now my eye sees you;
> therefore I despise myself,
>   and repent in dust and ashes." (Job 42:1-6)

As we read the Bible, it is striking to see that the most common way God gets the attention of His people is by referring them to His creative output.

> By the word of the Lord the heavens were made,
>   and by the breath of his mouth all their host.
> He gathers the waters of the sea as a heap;
>   he puts the deeps in storehouses.
> Let all the earth fear the Lord;
>   let all the inhabitants of the world stand in awe of him!
> For he spoke, and it came to be;
>   he commanded, and it stood firm. (Psalm 33:6-9)

Once we recognize that we are characters in a story we didn't write, we will also recognize that our attempts at rebellious rewriting are nothing compared to the classic literature in which we find ourselves.

Someone far greater than us wields the pen and will write the ending to our stories, so we had best understand our roles with fear and trembling so that we are not written out of His "happily ever after." When we deny the author of our salvation and start writing our own lines, we make ourselves into gods. And gods must be worshipped, so we offer ourselves sex, money, and power and end up filling our temples with money-changers and prostitutes. And then our personally penned autobiographies become nothing but pornographic pulp fiction.

> Therefore God gave them up in the lusts of their hearts to impurity, to the dishonoring of their bodies among themselves, because they exchanged the truth about God for a lie and worshiped and served the creature rather than the Creator, who is blessed forever! Amen. (Romans 1:24–25)

CHAPTER 5

Hearing Loss

Bridge of Sighs

Unfortunately, this bridge of divine discourse suffered structural damage during the Fall and became a *bridge of sighs*. The original sin of trying to become God left us deaf to His words and caused us to defiantly march to the beat of our own drummers.

> In the pride of his face the wicked does not seek him;
> all his thoughts are, "There is no God." (Psalm 10:4)

The problem with the Fall was that it cut us off from God. Instead of fearing the Lord, obtaining wisdom, and rethinking His thoughts, we became foolish, feared no one, and pursued our own thoughts. We replaced God's truth with humankind's truth and ended up believing the serpent's lie.

> You will not surely die. For God knows that in the day you eat of it your eyes will be opened, and you will be like God, knowing good and evil. (Genesis 3:4–5)

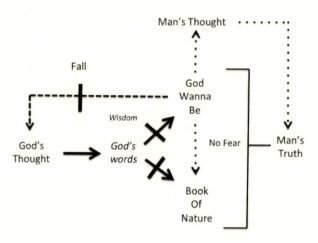

God created a perfect garden paradise and provided for Adam and Eve's every possible need. He offered them a full-time job and as much food as they could eat. He only asked that they avoid one particular tree because He knew that partaking of that fruit would change everything.

> The Lord God took the man and put him in the Garden of Eden to work it and keep it. And the Lord God commanded the man, saying, "You may surely eat of every tree of the garden, but of the tree of the knowledge of good and evil you shall not eat, for in the day that you eat of it you shall surely die." (Genesis 2:15–17)

God described the trees that humankind could eat from as "pleasant to the sight and good for food" (Genesis 2:9). However, when Eve was tempted with the tree of knowledge of good and evil, she saw one additional benefit.

> So when the woman saw that the tree was good for food, and that it was a delight to the eyes, *and that the tree was to be desired to make one wise,* she took of its fruit and ate, and she also gave some to her husband who was with her, and he ate. (Genesis 3:6, emphasis added)

Adam and Eve were tempted away from God's wisdom by the opportunity to acquire their own. Reality would now conform to their thoughts and not the original thought of God; they would exchange the truth (reality conforming to God's thought) for a lie (reality conforming to human thought). A lie is merely a misrepresentation of reality that results in faulty thinking; therefore, Satan wanted Adam and Eve to think the world was their oyster when it was actually God's pearl of great price. Instead of using a sacred sextant to align the heavens and the earth, they relied on a human compass that pointed only to themselves. Satan is in the business of misinformation, and he frequently deceives us by showering, shaving, and putting on a respectable angel-of-light persona; but we must always be on the lookout for his five-o'clock shadow of darkness.

In the beginning, Adam and Eve delighted in a world held together by God's wisdom, but once they succumbed to temptation, they watched in horror as the world fell apart under the supervision of their newly acquired devilish discernment. Adam and Eve felt like God was holding out on them, and in reality, He was, but what He withheld was disaster. We see this played out in our own lives when our teenagers bristle at our warnings because they feel like they are being denied the forbidden fruit of adulthood when we are really just trying to spare them from the indigestion that inevitably comes when people "eat of the apple, so young."[20] The first couple, in true teenage fashion, ignored their Father and ended up with a terminal case of "trespass tourista."

> Here again is the great irony of the Fall: attempting to make themselves into God, Adam and Eve become a pathetic parody of God, something like the tri-headed Satan of Dante; hoping to find security in self-sufficiency, they found only greater terror.[21]

The truth of each worldview can be determined by its ability to match thought with reality, and since we have already shown that a mind is responsible for the creation of the world, we must determine whether our interpretation of reality corresponds to His thought or our own. Since we are all reading from the same book of nature, we need to ask ourselves if we are acknowledging the author or writing our own story. Are we rethinking His thoughts or our own? Do we shape our own reality or live in God's reality? Do we create a space in which to live or live in a space created for us?

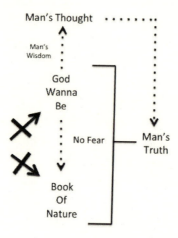

For although they knew God, they did not honor him as God or give thanks to him, but they became futile in their thinking, and their foolish hearts were darkened. *Claiming to be wise,* they became fools, and exchanged the glory of the immortal God for images resembling mortal man and birds and animals and reptiles ... because *they exchanged the truth about God for a lie* and worshiped and served the creature rather than the Creator, who is blessed forever! Amen. (Romans 1:21–23, 25, emphasis added)

You felt secure in your wickedness,
    you said, "No one sees me";
your wisdom and your knowledge led you astray,
and you said in your heart,
    "I am, and there is no one besides me." (Isaiah 47:10)

If you *believe you are God*, truth will be the correspondence of reality to *your thought*.

If you *believe in God*, truth will be the correspondence of reality to *His thought*.

Jesus, the Godly Grammarian

If our problem is reliance on our own faulty reasoning instead of God's preexistent wisdom, then how can we fix the problem? We have talked about the need to fear God in order to obtain wisdom, but we also need to recognize that original sin has so blinded us that we think we are the ones to be feared. We have taken the words God so eloquently spoke and scrambled them beyond recognition by attempting to be the authors of our own stories. We have confused the image with the image bearer and begun to believe our own press, and our autobiographies have become hagiographies. What we need is a refresher course in godly grammar. We need the teacher to step into our world classroom and give us another lesson in *Lingua Dei* 101.

> In the beginning was the Word, and the Word was with God, and the Word was God. He was in the beginning with God. All things were made through him, and without him was not anything made that was made.… And the Word became flesh and dwelt among us, and we have seen his glory, glory as of the only Son from the Father, full of grace and truth. (John 1:1–3, 14)

God spoke through His created words, and then He spoke through His prophets, but now He speaks definitively through His Son, the ultimate Word.

> Long ago, at many times and in many ways, God *spoke* to our fathers by the prophets, but in these last days

> he has *spoken* to us by his Son, whom he appointed the heir of all things, through whom also he created the world. He is the radiance of the glory of God and the exact imprint of his nature, and he upholds the universe by the *word* of his power. (Hebrews 1:1–3, emphasis added)

The trajectory of our original sin plot line would ultimately end with our doing away with God and assuming His throne. Jesus took our sinful rewrite to its natural conclusion and died on a cross, but then He did the unexpected and got us back on script by rising from the dead. Our story revision died on a Roman cross, but in reality, God's story had just begun. In a brilliant plot twist, the author emptied himself and became a character in His own salvation story in order to get us all on the same page.

> He is the image of the invisible God, the firstborn of all creation. For by him all things were created, in heaven and on earth, visible and invisible, whether thrones or dominions or rulers or authorities—all things were created through him and for him. And he is before all things, and in him all things hold together. And he is the head of the body, the church. He is the beginning, the firstborn from the dead, that in everything he might be preeminent. For in him all the fullness of God was pleased to dwell, and through him to reconcile to himself all things, whether on earth or in heaven, making peace by the blood of his cross. (Colossians 1:15–20)

Jesus is described as the wisdom of God, so what kind of fear do we need to have in order to obtain the wisdom of Jesus? Our redemptive fear begins by recognizing the immense gap between a Holy God and a sinful people. Jesus then helps us understand the extent of this gap by becoming the tape measure of salvation, gauging the distance from the right hand of God to the depths of human depravity. The life, death, and resurrection of Jesus add another dimension to what it means to fear the Lord. Fear not only includes the frightful distance between God and humankind but also the depths to which God would descend in order to bring them together. God's incarnation and death seem like extreme foolishness to the world but in reality were the most awesome manifestation of the wisdom of God.

> For the word of the cross is folly to those who are perishing, but to us who are being saved it is the power of God. For it is written, "I will destroy the wisdom of the wise, and the discernment of the discerning I will thwart." Where is the one who is wise? Where is the scribe? Where is the debater of this age? Has not God made foolish the wisdom of the world? For since, in the wisdom of God, the world did not know God through wisdom, it pleased God through the folly of what we preach to save those who believe. For Jews demand signs and Greeks seek wisdom, but we preach Christ crucified, a stumbling block to Jews and folly to Gentiles, but to those who are called, both Jews and Greeks, *Christ the power of God and the wisdom of God*. For the foolishness of God is wiser than men, and the weakness of God is stronger than men. For consider your calling, brothers: not many of you were wise according to worldly standards, not many were powerful, not many were of noble birth. But God chose what is foolish in the world to shame the wise; God chose what is weak in the world to shame the strong; God chose what is low and despised in the world, even things that are not, to bring to nothing things that are, so that no human being might boast in the presence of God. *He is the source of your life in Christ Jesus, whom God made our wisdom and our righteousness and sanctification and redemption.* Therefore, as it is written, "Let the one who boasts, boast in the Lord." (1 Corinthians 1:18–31, emphasis added)

The fear of the Lord is most powerfully displayed on the cross, where the absolute holiness of God intersects with the absolute sinfulness of humankind. The amazing thing is that this chasm of fear becomes filled with a resurrection of hope. Jesus transforms the fear of what we cannot accomplish ourselves into awe of what God has done on our behalf. When we accept Christ, we can once again participate in the wisdom of God and be led into all truth. Through Jesus, we once again become the image bearers God had intended from the beginning.

Jesus is also called truth because He is the perfect physical representation of God's thought. When we seek Jesus, we are ultimately trying to know God's thoughts through His perfect Word. Jesus is wisdom, truth, the Word, and the perfect image of God; therefore, He is the only one able to restore the perfect correspondence between God's thoughts and His world.

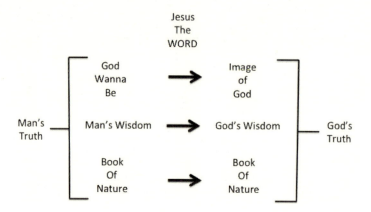

Beloved, do not believe every spirit, but test the spirits to see whether they are from God, for many false prophets have gone out into the world. By this you know the Spirit of God: every spirit that confesses that Jesus Christ has come in the flesh is from God, and every spirit that does not confess Jesus is not from God. (1 John 4:1–3)

CHAPTER 6
The Final Word

Most of us recognize that the physical world speaks to us in spiritual ways. The very fact that we bend our ears to listen implies that "it" must have something to say. This spirit wants to share a thought with us, not as a lecture but rather as a dialogue—not as polite pleasantries but as a partnership. While a small group of vocal atheists tries to convince us that these spiritual longings are nothing but chemicals fearing the unknown, it is the mystical musings of the majority of us that drive our insatiable desire to find this spirit. While this universal desire unites us, our conclusions divide us. We all have the same God-shaped hole, but the odd ways in which we try to fill it create religious differences. Our postmodern culture admirably tries to bring harmony to the situation by telling us that all paths lead to the same divine mountaintop, but that illusory unity is shattered once we reach the summit and look around to see that each religious victory flag has been stuck on a completely different peak. Religion unites us not because our paths end with the same God but because they all begin with the same spiritual hole. We are empty because our souls are lonely and need a spiritual spouse; therefore, proper religious seeking comes down to finding Mr. Right and not pursuing idolatrous one-night stands.

In order to begin our celestial search, we must first check our divine pretensions at the door and recognize that the original sin of thinking that we are gods has short-circuited our efforts to find this spirit. Sadly, we usually begin by creating gods in our own image, not because we lack divine information, but because we lack mortal humility. We then exchange the truth for a lie and set up a puppet deity so we can pull our own strings. The problem is that once we place ourselves in the divine driver's seat and our lives spin out of control, we can't help but cry out, "Jesus, take the wheel," because deep down we know we have been driving with a suspended license ever since we wrapped ourselves around that particular tree in the garden of Eden. It's easy to worship the god *within* when our lives are rosy, but when we feel the sting of the thorns and thistles, we have no choice but to turn to the God *without*.

St. Paul couldn't have made it any clearer when he wrote to the Roman Christians and told them that they were "without excuse" for not knowing the one true God, because the physical world was constantly speaking to them of spiritual things. While these early Christians had no excuse, we have even fewer because the once-simple vocabulary of the natural world has become exceedingly complex due to our scientific advances, and that once *still, small voice* has been amplified by the megaphone of biological information and design. Atheists tell us to ignore the "signature in the cell" because they can't seem to see the divine writing on the biological wall. They are then left with a chemical conundrum because the spirit they crave is reduced to an enzyme facilitating a reaction rather than a being who has lovingly spoken. Albert Einstein found it remarkable that the world was mathematically comprehensible, but we Christians just consider it a daily conversation with God.

The ability of a spirit to speak to us in physical terms is not without precedence in our daily lives. Our daily acts of communication prove that the immaterial can become material every time our thoughts become speech. We are then forced to ask ourselves which worldview recognizes speech as the perfect bridge between the sacred and secular. The good news is that the God of the Bible comprehensively embraces divine discourse through His creational *words*, His written *Word*, and His incarnate *WORD*. Since life is so complex and we humans have so many questions, it is comforting to know that we have a God who is not afraid to speak His mind. The real issue is whether we will listen or brazenly put words into His mouth.

While it is amazing that God speaks, it is even more amazing that there are beings on this planet who can understand what He has spoken. Once again, the Bible gives us insight by explaining that we are created in His image and therefore perfectly designed to hear what He has to say. We recognize our Father's voice because we are His offspring. Our unique ability to hear God's words, however, comes with some significant responsibility because it demands a response. We can't wait until the end of our lives to complain that He didn't make a peep, because He will just turn around and say, "I spoke daily. Why were you unwilling to listen?"

God calls us to worship Him in spirit and truth, so we are commanded to fact-check all His truth claims. Since truth is the correlation of thought and reality, we can look at the world around us and compare it to His scriptural thoughts. We can match His general revelation with His special revelation and see if we have a *word*, for *Word*, for *WORD* correspondence. This, however, is no easy task because the hurricane-force winds of the Fall caused the tree of the knowledge of good and evil to fall and damage the lines of communication with God. We have become sinfully schizophrenic and are unable to discern between His voice and the voices in our heads, so we end up transforming God into a dummy for our vain ventriloquism. It is not hopeless, however, because for those who sincerely want to hear His voice, He gives access to a wisdom signal-booster to cut through all the cultural white noise and get better reception. This wisdom, though, is only available if we stand in awe of the rhetorical power of His creational speech. *We must fear before we can hear.* Thankfully, God sent His only begotten *WORD*, the perfect combination of the spiritual and the physical, the transcendent and the immanent, and the immaterial and the material so that, hearing, we can now truly hear.

We can't let the world pull up the drawbridge between the sacred and the secular, because we are dependent on the goods and services that only come from the mouth of the Lord. If we interrupt this divine commerce, we will *surely die* of spiritual malnutrition. God has spoken;

therefore, we have only two choices: we can either hang on His every word and venture across the bridge of divine discourse, or we can love the sound of our own voices and become prisoners of our human vocabulary.

ENDNOTES

Chapter One

1. Frank Newport, "Most Americans Still Believe in God," *Gallup News*, June 29, 2016, http://news.gallup.com/poll/193271/americans-believe-god.aspx.
2. Barna Group, "Competing Worldviews Influence Today's Christians," May 2017, https://www.barna.com/research/competing-worldviews-influence-todays-christians/.
3. Pew Research Center, "U.S. Public Becoming Less Religious," November 2015, http://www.pewforum.org/2015/11/03/u-s-public-becoming-less-religious/
4. Taken from my blog entitled, The Divine Void, written Dec. 30, 2015. http://www.godsscreenplay.com/the-divine-void/
5. I cover this in much more detail in my book *Cry of the Elephant Man: Listening for Man's Voice above the Herd* (Bloomington, IN: WestBow Press, 2016).
6. Sir James Jeans, Simple to Remember.com, http://www.simpletoremember.com/articles/a/science-quotes/.

Chapter Two

7. C. S. Lewis, *The Screwtape Letters* (New York: Time Inc., 1963), 24–25. God is referred to as the enemy because the book is a series of correspondences between a junior devil-in-training and his supervisor discussing the best ways to corrupt humankind.

Chapter Three

8. Albert Einstein quoted at BrainyQuote, https://www.brainyquote.com/quotes/quotes/a/alberteins125369.html.
9. "If a Tree Falls in a Forest," Wikipedia.com, https://en.wikipedia.org/wiki/If_a_tree_falls_in_a_forest.
10. Deborah Kelemen, "Are Children Intuitive Theists: Reasoning about Purpose and Design in Nature," *Psychological Science* 15, no. 5 (2004): 295–301.
11. Justin L. Barrett, *Born Believers: The Science of Children's Religious Belief* (New York: Free Press, 2012).

12. "Understanding the Hebrew Word for 'Listen' Will Change Your Relationship with God," Churchleaders.com, April 2017, http://churchleaders.com/pastors/videos-for-pastors/301627-understanding-hebrew-word-listen-will-change-relationship-god.html.
13. MIT News, "Chomsky Explores Origins of Language," April 1992, http://news.mit.edu/1992/chomsky-0401.
14. Douglas Axe, *Undeniable: How Biology Confirms Our Intuition That Life Is Designed* (New York: HarperCollins, 2016), 259–260.
15. I cover this in much more detail in my book *The Director's Cut: Finding God's Screenplay on the Cutting Room Floor* (Bloomington, IN: WestBow Press, 2014).
16. Simone Weil, quoted in Phillip Yancey, *Soul Survivor* (New York: Galilee/Doubleday, 2001), 262.

Chapter Four

17. Thomas Aquinas, *Summa Theologiae* (Question 16, article 2), http://www.newadvent.org/summa/1016.htm.
18. Mortimer Adler, "Six Great Ideas: The Liar and the Skeptic," Jesusi, http://cyberspacei.com/greatbooks/h2/6gi/gi_005.htm.
19. Blue Letter Bible. https://www.blueletterbible.org/lang/lexicon/lexicon.cfm?Strongs=H7832&t=ESV

Chapter Five

20. Alice in Chains, "Rotten Apple," *Jar of Flies*, Sony Legacy, 1994.
21. Robert Barron, *And Now I See* (New York: Crossroad, 1998), 94.

Made in United States
North Haven, CT
05 January 2024